W9-DEF-487

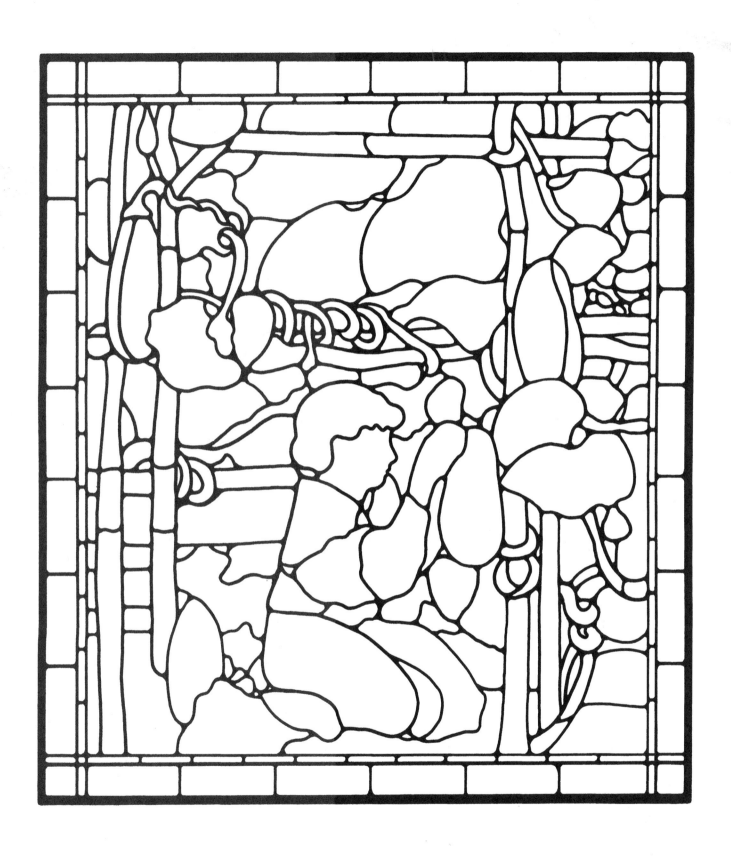

Girl Picking Gourds, 1890's, living room at Laurelton Hall, Oyster Bay, NY.

Domestic floral window of trellised trumpet vines, date unknown.

La Moisson Fleurie (Harvest in Bloom), one of two windows designed by Paul Ranson and executed by Tiffany, New York, displayed Paris 1895.

Landscape window (detail), 1908–1912.

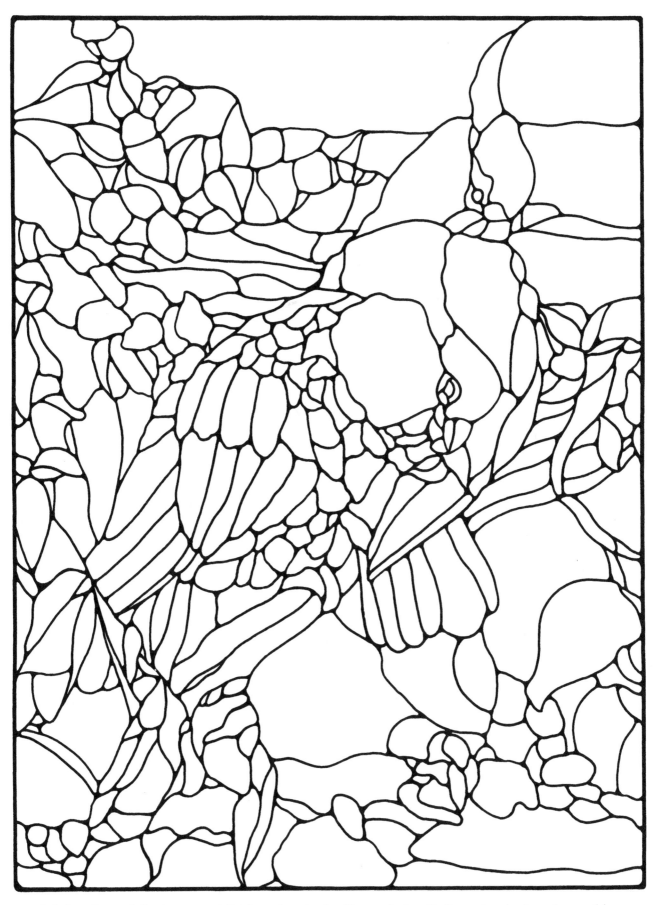

Sulphur Crested Cockatoos, exhibition piece in the Haworth Art Gallery, Accrington, Lancashire, date unknown.

Bamboo Panel, date unknown.

Landscape with Birches, date unknown.

The Lucien and Julia Barnes Memorial in the Pilgrim Congregational Church, Duluth, Minnesota, 1930.

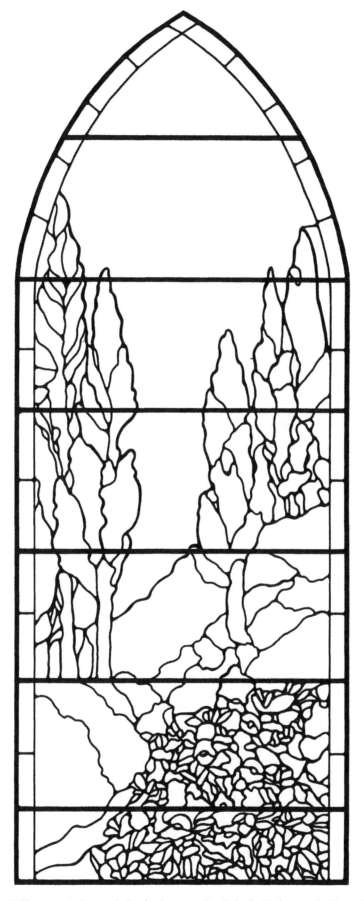

The Frederick A. Wilcoxon Memorial window at St. John's Episcopal Church, North Adams, Massachusetts, 1910.

Tiffany glass screen, 1902.

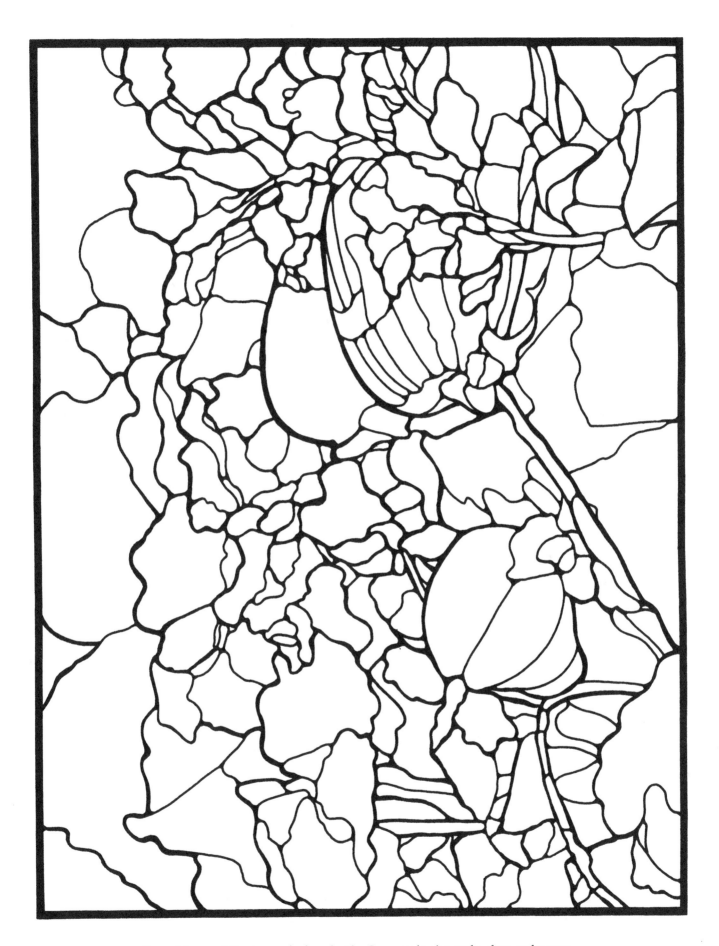

Pumpkins and Beets, a window in the Impressionist style, date unknown.

Sunrise, the first of a pair of memorial windows, 1918.

Sunset, the second of a pair of memorial windows, 1918.

The Deep Sea, designed by Tiffany and exhibited at the Libre Esthétique, Brussels, 1897.

Autumn, designed by Lydia Emmet, 1893.

The Edith and Edward Darling Memorial window in Bay Head, New Jersey, c. 1904.

A domestic window, date unknown.

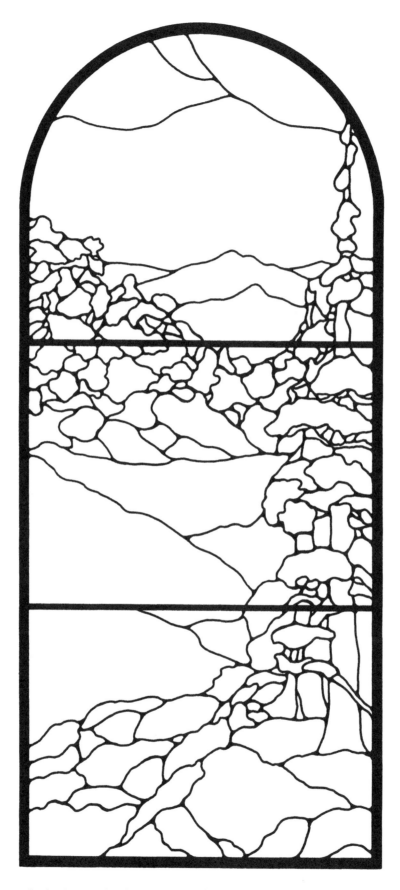

Rest, one of five panels depicting the four seasons, in Battell Chapel, Church of Christ Congregational, Norfolk, Connecticut, date unknown.

Charles Duncan and William G. Hegardt Memorial window in the Pilgrim Congregational Church, Duluth, Minnesota, c. 1924.

Detail of Charles Duncan and William G. Hegardt Memorial window, c. 1924.

Wisteria transom, date unknown.

Landscape window, one of Tiffany's later works, c. 1920.

Landscape window, c. 1912.

Memorial window (detail) in the Third Presbyterian Church, Rochester, New York, 1902.

Detail of Magnolia panel designed by Agnes Northrop.

The Julia Wheeler Tiffany Memorial window in St. James Episcopal Church, Fordham, New York.

The Julia Wheeler Tiffany Memorial window, detail of left side.

The Julia Wheeler Tiffany Memorial window, detail of right side.

Landscape memorial window designed by Agnes Northrop.

A domestic panel with parrots and hibiscus; date unknown.

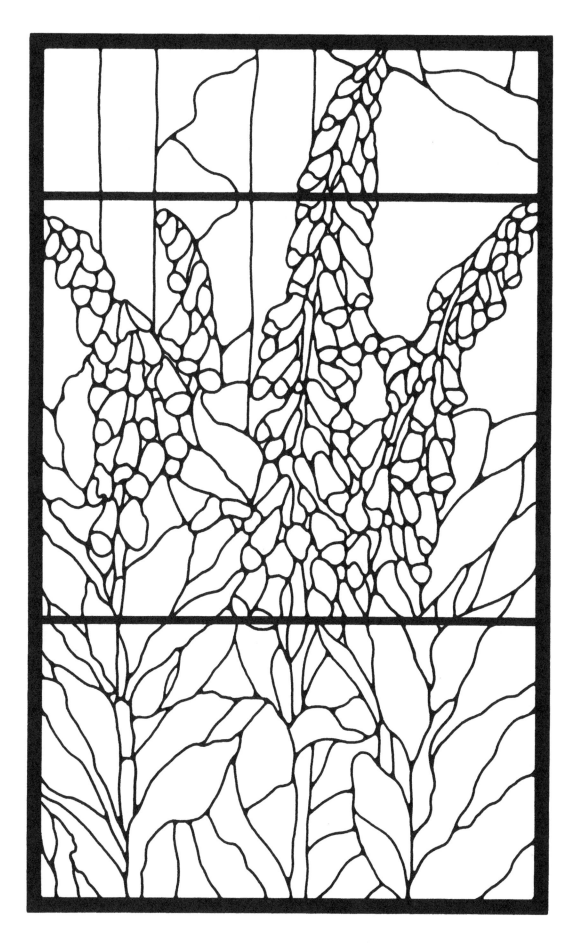

Detail of triptych in St. James Country Club, Perryopolis, Pennsylvania.

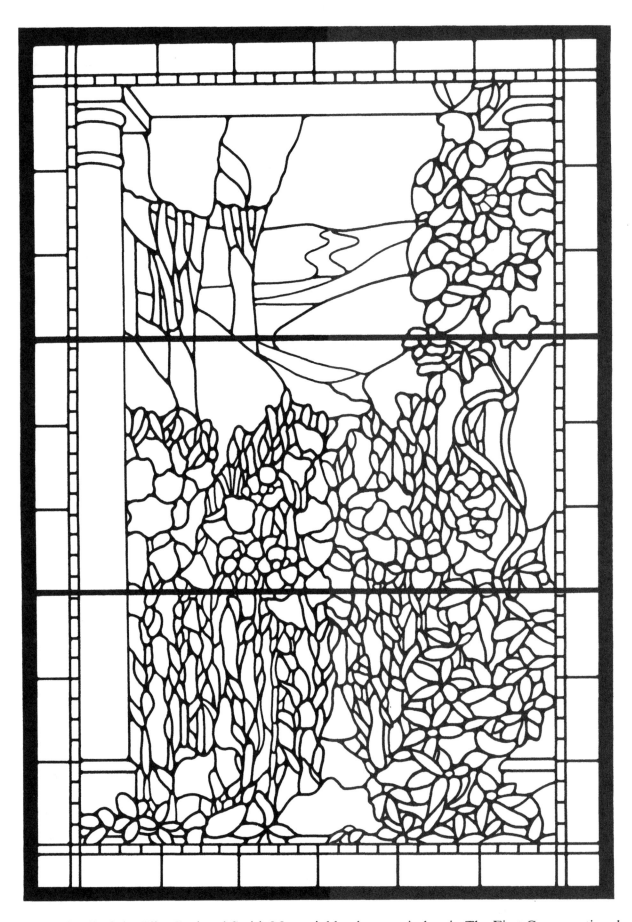

Peace, detail of the Eliza Brainerd Smith Memorial landscape window in The First Congregational Church, St. Albans, Vermont, c. 1905.

Easter lilies, firescreen, one of three panels, 1910.

Passion flower floral window, detail.

The Frank Memorial window, date unknown.

Landscape window, date unknown.

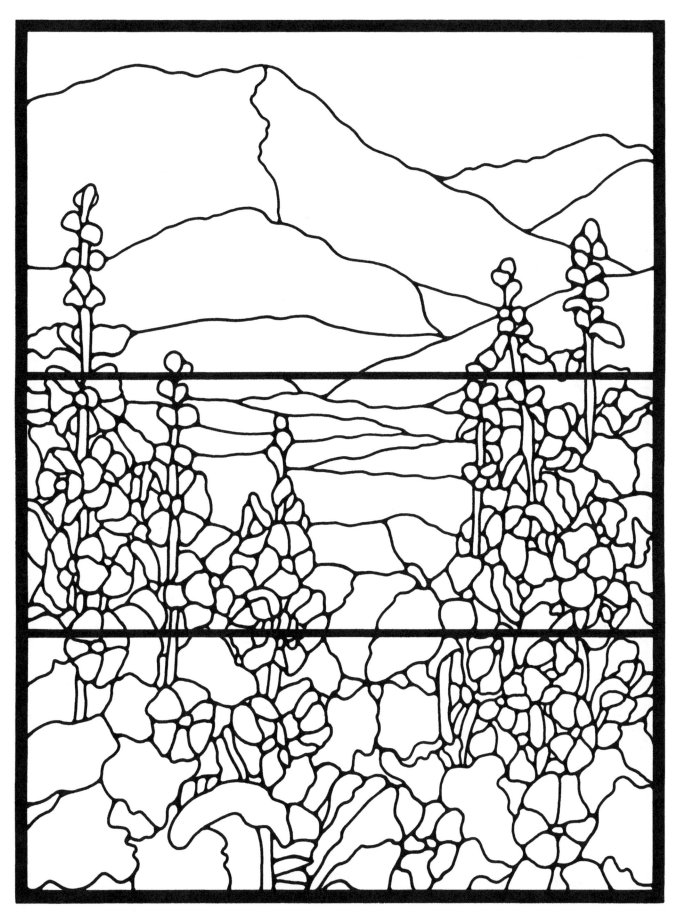

Domestic landscape triptych with hollyhocks (detail), date unknown.

The Frederick Henry Betts Memorial window, St. Andrews Dune Church,
Southampton, Long Island, c. 1906.

Peacock window, c. 1910.

The Allen Parkhill Northrop Memorial window (detail), in the Reformed Church, Flushing, Long Island, 1903.

The Lauriston Livingston Stone Memorial window, 1920.

"Sir Galahad," the Ogden Cryder Memorial window in St. Andrew's Dune Church, Southampton, Long Island, 1902.

The Maria Louise Beebe Memorial window in the YWCA, 53rd Street and Lexington Avenue, New York City, 1917.

The Sarah Gibbs Thompson Memorial window (detail), *Recreation and Music,* designed by
Frederick Thompson and installed in the Postgraduate Hospital, New York City, 1899.

The Sarah Gibbs Thompson Memorial window (detail).

The Minnie Proctor Memorial window (left panel detail), 1928.

The Minnie Proctor Memorial window (right panel detail).

Morning Glories, memorial window (detail) in the Unitarian Church, Northampton, Massachusetts, c. 1905.

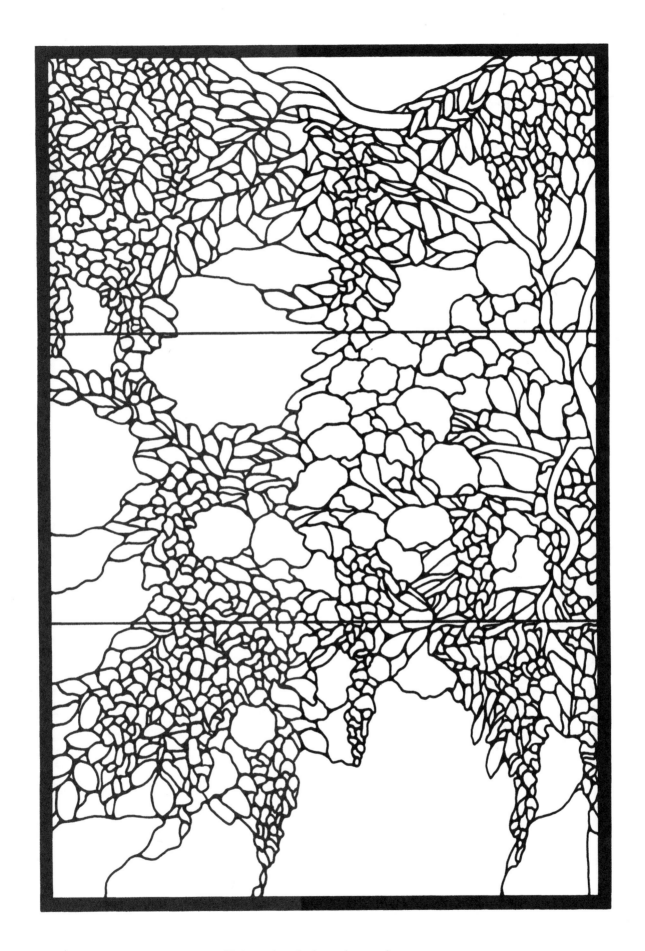

Domestic window, date unknown.

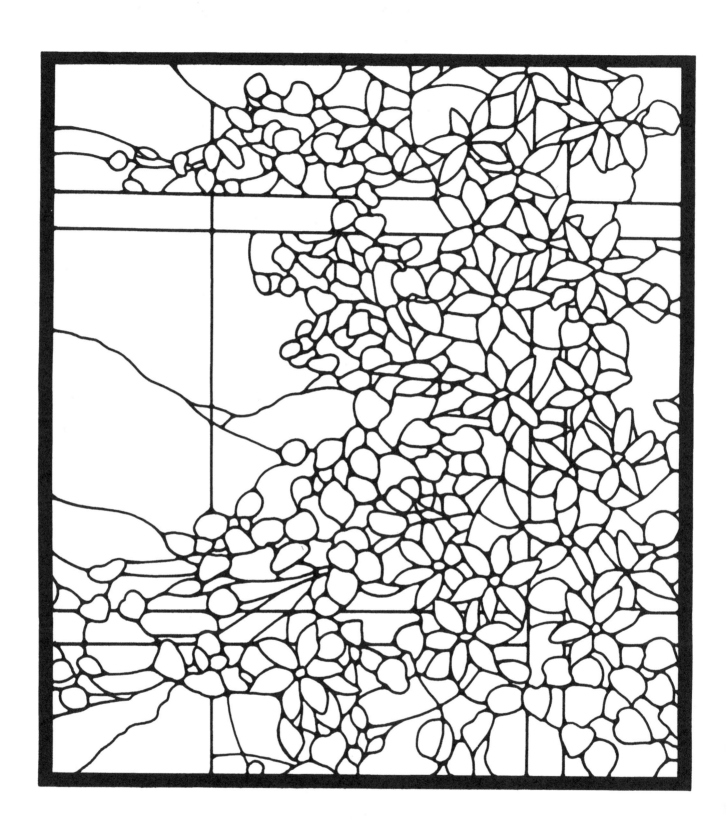

Floral skylight, c. 1912.

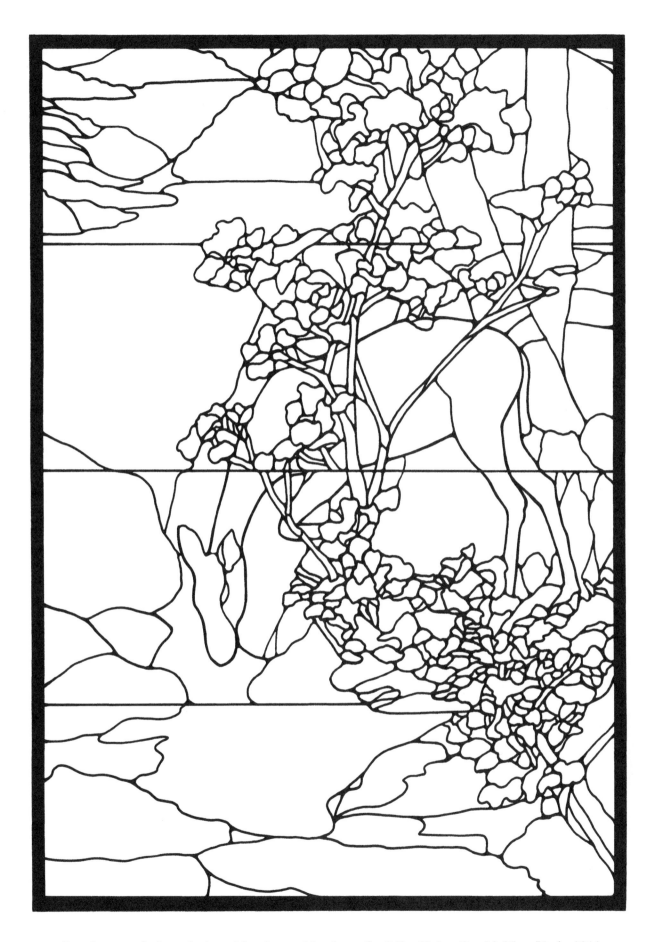

Landscape window, designed by Agnes Northrop for Miss Helen Gould, New York, 1911.

Detail of window for the stairway of the Richard B. Mellon house, Pittsburgh, 1908–1912.

The Hector, detail of the T. R. Trowbridge Memorial in The First Church of Christ,
New Haven, Connecticut, 1898.

Parrots, detail of window commissioned by Captain Joseph R. Delmar, New York, c. 1912.

The Greysolon Duluth Memorial window (detail), 1904.

Detail of landscape window commissioned by Richard B. Mellon for the stairway landing of his house in Pittsburgh, 1908–1912.

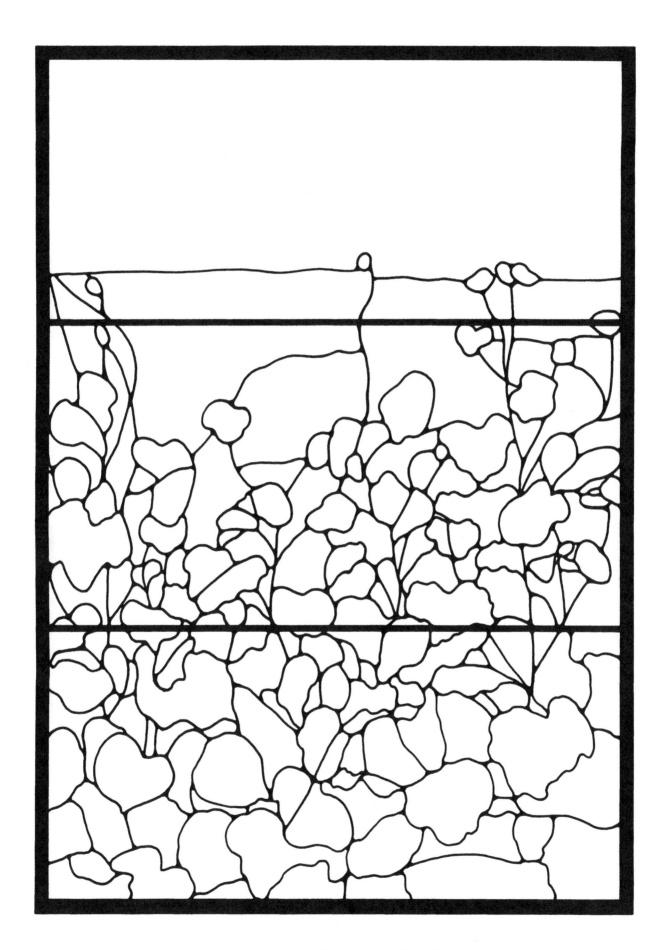

Richard B. Mellon window (detail).

Richard B. Mellon window (detail).

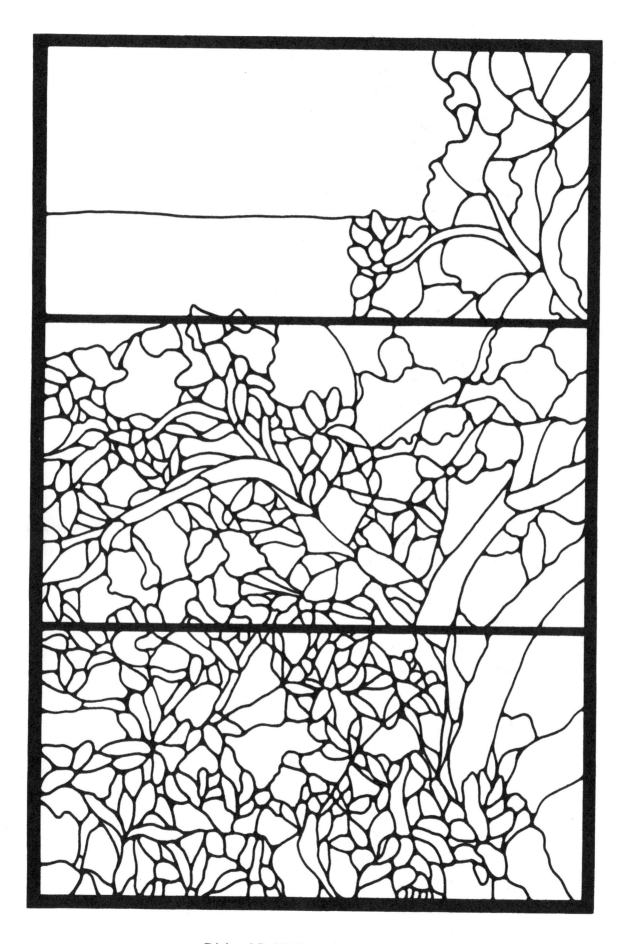

Richard B. Mellon window (detail).

Detail of landscape window commissioned by Webb Horton for the stairway in his forty room mansion in Middletown, New York, 1902.

TIFFANY WINDOWS
Stained Glass Pattern Book

Connie Eaton

DOVER PUBLICATIONS, INC.
Mineola, New York

Copyright

Copyright © 1997 by Dover Publications, Inc.
All rights reserved.

Bibliographical Note

Tiffany Windows is a new work, first published by
Dover Publications, Inc., in 1997.

International Standard Book Number

ISBN-13: 978-0-486-29853-5
ISBN-10: 0-486-29853-1

Manufactured in the United States by LSC Communications
29853113   2017
www.doverpublications.com

PUBLISHER'S NOTE

Louis Comfort Tiffany (1848–1933) was a pioneer of modern design. Originally trained as a painter, Tiffany loved the unique qualities of glass, and was attracted to the idea that work in glass could be functional as well as beautiful. Tiffany began experimenting with glass in 1875, and by the 1890's had produced an inimitable glass he called *favrile*, which was iridescent, freely textured, and was often combined with metal alloys for shimmering effects. Influenced by William Morris, whose work had launched the Arts and Crafts movement, Tiffany wished to render figures in stained glass windows without the use of brush work. His stained glass demonstrates an arts-and-crafts conscience in its respect for materials, and a wish to transform the way Americans thought about the function of art in the home.

The sixty designs included in this book are accurate representations of original Tiffany designs. Although these stained glass designs are intended for craftspeople already familiar with the basics of the craft, the patterns will have many applications, depending on the needs and imagination of the individual putting them to use. Instructions on selecting and cutting glass are not provided here, but those not familiar with these skills may want to refer to *Stained Glass Craft* by J. A. F. Divine and G. Blachford, Dover Publications, 0-486-22812-6.